# WORLD ALMANAC®
## LIBRARY OF THE STATES

# Oklahoma

## THE SOONER STATE

*by Michael Martin*

Curriculum Consultant: Jean Craven,
Director of Instructional Support,
Albuquerque, NM, Public Schools

**WORLD ALMANAC® LIBRARY**

Please visit our web site at: **www.worldalmanaclibrary.com**
For a free color catalog describing World Almanac® Library's
list of high-quality books and multimedia programs, call
1-800-848-2928 (USA) or 1-800-387-3178 (Canada).
World Almanac® Library's fax: (414) 332-3567.

**Library of Congress Cataloging-in-Publication Data**

Martin, Michael A.
    Oklahoma, the Sooner State / by Michael A. Martin.
       p. cm. — (World Almanac Library of the states)
    Includes bibliographical references and index.
    Summary: Describes the history, geography, government, culture, people,
and special events and attractions of the state of Oklahoma.
    ISBN 0-8368-5142-0 (lib. bdg.)
    ISBN 0-8368-5312-1 (softcover)
    1. Oklahoma—Juvenile literature. [1. Oklahoma.] I. Title. II. Series.
F694.3.M37   2002
976.6—dc21                          2002074270

This edition first published in 2002 by
**World Almanac® Library**
330 West Olive Street, Suite 100
Milwaukee, WI 53212 USA

This edition © 2002 by World Almanac® Library.

Design and Editorial: Bill SMITH STUDIO Inc.
Editor: Timothy Paulson
Assistant Editor: Megan Elias
Art Director: Olga Lamm
Photo Research: Sean Livingstone
World Almanac® Library Project Editor: Patricia Lantier
World Almanac® Library Editors: Monica Rausch, Jacqueline Laks Gorman, Mary Dykstra
World Almanac® Library Production: Tammy Gruenewald, Katherine A. Goedheer

Photo credits: pp. 4-5 © Fred W. Marvel/Oklahoma Tourism; p. 6 (top) © PhotoDisc, (bottom)
© Corel; p. 7 (top) © Corel, (bottom) © Fred W. Marvel/Oklahoma Tourism; p. 9 © ArtToday;
p. 10 © Baldwin H. Ward & Kathryn C. Ward/CORBIS; p. 11 Denver Public Library; p. 12
© Library of Congress; pp. 12-13 © Library of Congress; p. 14 © Library of Congress; p. 15
© Fred W. Marvel/Oklahoma Tourism; p. 17 © Library of Congress; p. 18 © PhotoDisc; p. 19
Denver Public Library; p. 20 (left to right) © Corel, © Fred W. Marvel/Oklahoma Tourism,
© Fred W. Marvel/Oklahoma Tourism; p. 21 (all) © Fred W. Marvel/Oklahoma Tourism; p. 23
© Fred W. Marvel/Oklahoma Tourism; p. 26 (top) © PhotoDisc, (bottom) © PhotoDisc; pp. 26-27
© Library of Congress; p. 29 © Fred W. Marvel/Oklahoma Tourism; p. 31 © Library of Congress;
p. 33 (all) © Fred W. Marvel/Oklahoma Tourism; p. 34 © Martha Swope/TimePix; p. 35 © Fred W.
Marvel/Oklahoma Tourism; p. 36 © Fred W. Marvel/Oklahoma Tourism; p. 37 © Fred W.
Marvel/Oklahoma Tourism; p. 38 © Library of Congress; p. 39 © PhotoDisc; p. 40 © NASA; p. 41
© PhotoDisc; pp. 42-43 © Library of Congress; p. 44 © Fred W. Marvel/Oklahoma Tourism; p. 45
(top) © Fred W. Marvel/Oklahoma Tourism, (bottom) © PhotoDisc

Printed in the United States of America

1 2 3 4 5 6 7 8 9 06 05 04 03 02

# Oklahoma

# Crossroads of the West

Sitting astride the rugged Ouachita Mountains, the hilly Ozark Plateau, and the southern extent of North America's Great Plains, Oklahoma's landscape is varied and colorful — and the same can be said of its history, culture, and people. The U.S. government first relocated Native Americans here from points east. Later, the area became the domain of hardy pioneers. These settlers would, in a few short years, turn Oklahoma's grass-covered prairies into a vast patchwork of farms, cattle ranches, small towns, and sprawling cities.

Oklahoma was one of the last continental U.S. territories to achieve statehood. Although its life as a state began in 1907, Oklahoma became critically important to the nation during the several decades that preceded statehood. Blessed with an abundance of fertile agricultural soils and fossil fuel deposits, Oklahoma has long served the nation as both breadbasket and powerhouse. But the Sooner State has given the world more than food and fuel — it is also the birthplace of some of the nation's most accomplished artists and athletes. Oklahoma's lengthy roll call of distinguished natives includes folk singer Woody Guthrie, novelist Ralph Ellison, dancer Maria Tallchief, baseball great Mickey Mantle, cartoonist Chester Gould, and astronaut Shannon Lucid.

Oklahoma encompasses buffalo-trod plains and granite mountains, mighty rivers and gypsum hills, cacti and pines. It is a place where diverse landforms, as well as people, meet and mingle. It is a land of enduring Native cultures and high-tech industries, of modern-day powwows and competitive rodeos — the real-world West so long romanticized by Hollywood. Oklahoma symbolizes the exhilarating union of East and West, past and future.

▶ Map of Oklahoma showing the interstate highway system, as well as major cities and waterways.

▼ Black Mesa, Oklahoma's highest point, rises up from Cimarron County in the western region of the state.

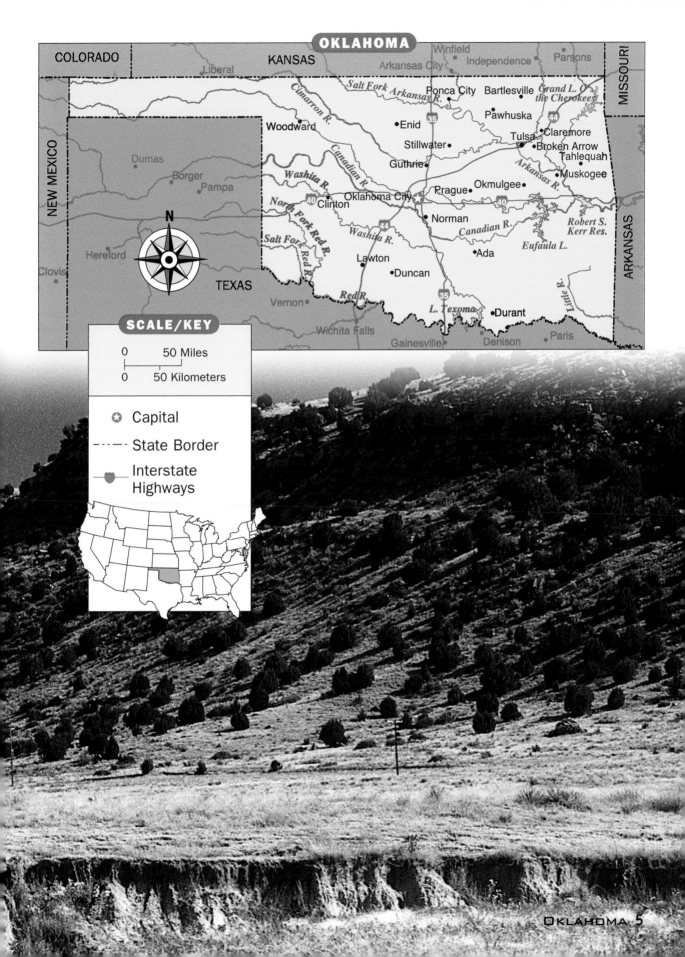

# OKLAHOMA

COLORADO

KANSAS

MISSOURI

NEW MEXICO

ARKANSAS

TEXAS

Liberal

Winfield

Arkansas City

Independence

Parsons

Salt Fork Arkansas R.

Ponca City

Bartlesville

Grand L. O' the Cherokees

Woodward

Dumas

Borger

Pampa

Cimarron R.

Canadian R.

Enid

Pawhuska

44

Stillwater

Tulsa

Claremore

Washita R.

Guthrie

Broken Arrow

Tahlequah

North Fork Red R.

40

Clinton

Oklahoma City

Prague

Okmulgee

Arkansas R.

Muskogee

Salt Fork Red R.

Washita R.

44

Norman

Canadian R.

Robert S. Kerr Res.

Hereford

Clovis

Ada

Eufaula L.

Lawton

Duncan

35

L. Texoma

Durant

Little R.

Vernon

Red R.

Wichita Falls

Gainesville

Denison

Paris

## SCALE/KEY

0    50 Miles

0    50 Kilometers

⭐ Capital

-··-··- State Border

🛡 Interstate Highways

# Fast Facts

**OKLAHOMA**

## OKLAHOMA (OK), The Sooner State, The Boomer State

**Entered Union**

November 16, 1907 (46th state)

| Capital | Population |
| --- | --- |
| Oklahoma City | 506,132 |

**Total Population (2000)**

3,450,654 (27th most populous state) — *Between 1990 and 2000, the population of Oklahoma increased 9.7 percent.*

| Largest Cities | Population |
| --- | --- |
| Oklahoma City | 506,132 |
| Tulsa | 393,049 |
| Norman | 95,694 |
| Lawton | 92,757 |
| Broken Arrow | 74,859 |

**Land Area**

68,667 square miles (177,847 square kilometers) (19th largest state)

**State Motto**

"Labor Omnia Vincit" — *Latin for* "Labor Conquers All Things"

**State Song**

"Oklahoma!" — *lyrics by Oscar Hammerstein II, music by Richard Rodgers, adopted in 1953. This song has been featured in the Broadway musical and movie of the same name.*

**State Animal**

American buffalo — *Also known as bison, these massive, brown, shaggy creatures can weigh up to 2,000 pounds (907 kilograms).*

**State Game Animal**

White-tailed deer

**State Fur-Bearing Animal**

Raccoon

**State Insect**

Honeybee

**State Beverage**

Milk — *The typical Oklahoma cow produces about 200,000 glasses of milk during its lifetime, which works out to around ninety 8-ounce (2.4-deciliter) glasses per day.*

**State Folk Dance**

Square dance

**State Butterfly**

Black swallowtail — *This common butterfly* (Papilio polyxenes) *has a black body with yellow spots along each side. Its wings are black with two bands of blue and yellow marks.*

**State Musical Instrument**

Fiddle — *This instrument has been a staple of entertainment and dances in Oklahoma since the first non-Native settlers began homesteading in the territory.*

**State Percussive Musical Instrument**

Drum — *The drum has been important to the culture and religion of Oklahoma's Native Americans since prehistoric times.*

## PLACES TO VISIT

**Cherokee Heritage Center,** *southeast of Tahlequah*
This Native American museum includes the Tsa-La-Gi Ancient Village, a reconstructed village from before the days of European contact. Members of the Cherokee (Keetoowha) Nation provide tours for visitors between May and September.

**Tom Mix Museum,** *Dewey*
Many fans of the legendary silent-movie cowboy Tom Mix consider this museum among the best of its kind. Among its many attractions is a life-size replica of Mix's costar, Tony the Wonder Horse.

**USS *Batfish* Submarine and Museum,** *Muskogee*
The USS *Batfish* is a genuine historical treasure, a real naval submarine that played an important role in the Allied victory in World War II. Now located on the grounds of Muskogee's War Memorial Park, the submarine is open to the public.

For other places and events, see p. 44.

## BIGGEST, BEST, AND MOST

- The Port of Catoosa, located northeast of Tulsa, is the nation's largest and most inland ice-free port. It is also the world's northernmost ice-free port.

- Oklahoma City rose from the prairie in a single day. On the morning of April 22, 1889, the land was uninhabited. By evening, more than ten thousand people had rushed to the site — the biggest population boom in history.

## STATE FIRSTS

- **1909** The first Boy Scout troop in the United States was formed in Pawhuska.

- **1935** Oklahoma City became the home of the first automatic parking meter on July 16.

- **1990** Oklahoma became the first state to pass term limits for elected officials.

## The Cow Chip Capital of the World

Every April, the town of Beaver hosts its annual World Championship Cow Chip Throw, during which enthusiastic competitors hurl Frisbee-like disks of sun-dried cow droppings. The distance record for a thrown cow chip, established in 1979, stands at 182.3 feet (55.6 meters). Between competitions, souvenir cow chips can be purchased in this extremely cattle-friendly city. The "Chip Toss" competition frequently receives national media attention. If you visit Beaver during chip-tossing season, be sure to duck — and don't forget to wipe your feet!

## They Grow 'em Big

The Golden Driller, or "Giant Oil Man" — also known as "Larry" and "Golden Boy" — has been standing in front of the International Petroleum Exhibition building at the Tulsa Fair Grounds since 1966. This yellow statue of an oil-field worker leaning on an oil derrick is 76 feet (23 m) tall and made of a steel frame covered in concrete and plaster. In 1970, Larry had to be dismantled to replace part of his back, which had become weak. The Golden Driller is Oklahoma's official state monument and is considered one of Tulsa's historic sites.

# The Land That Filled Up Fast

Many a page of life has turned
Many a lesson I have learned.
— from "Oklahoma Hills,"
by Woody Guthrie and Jack Guthrie, 1937

The sprawling plains of the land we now call Oklahoma were first inhabited by nomadic hunters somewhere between fifteen and eighteen thousand years ago. These Paleo-Indians followed the region's vast buffalo herds. Some lived in caves in western Oklahoma. Centuries passed, and by the time Europeans first entered the region, several Native American groups had moved in. Among these were the Arapaho, Caddo, Cheyenne, Comanche, Kiowa, Osage, Pawnee, Quapaw, and Wichita.

## European Exploration and Settlement

The region's first European explorer was Francisco Vásquez de Coronado of Spain, whose 1540–1541 expedition crossed into present-day Oklahoma during an unsuccessful quest for gold. By some accounts, Spanish explorer Hernando de Soto came through the region later, in 1541. Neither Coronado nor de Soto established a permanent settlement. It was not until 1817 that French explorer and fur trader Auguste Pierre Chouteau established Oklahoma's first permanent European settlement. His trading outpost was built on the site of present-day Salina.

## A Traded Territory

In 1762, France ceded much of its North American holdings — including the Oklahoma region — to Spain, but regained control of these lands in 1800. Although the United States purchased the Louisiana Territory from the French in 1803, expanding U.S. land holdings by more than 800,000 square miles (2 million sq km), it was not immediately clear whether or not this huge chunk of North America extended all the way to the Oklahoma region. The matter was not settled until 1819, when the Adams-Onis Treaty established

| Native Americans of Oklahoma (pre-European Contact) |
| --- |
| Arapaho |
| Caddo |
| Cheyenne |
| Comanche |
| Kiowa |
| Osage |
| Pawnee |
| Quapaw |
| Wichita |

**DID YOU KNOW?**

The name *Oklahoma* comes from two words in the Choctaw language: *okla*, which means "people," and *homma* (or *humma*), meaning "red."

the western and southern boundaries of the United States. Oklahoma's narrow, northwesterly section — called the Panhandle — lay beyond that frontier, under Spanish control.

Control of the Panhandle passed to Mexico in 1821, and then to the Republic of Texas in 1836. When Texas entered the Union in 1845, the Panhandle came under U.S. jurisdiction, although it was not part of any specific U.S. territory. (Oklahoma's boundaries did not assume their present shape until 1890, when the U.S. Congress created the Oklahoma Territory.)

After the Louisiana Purchase, European explorers and traders moved into the Oklahoma area. Goods bought from Native Americans were sent, via barges, from Oklahoma to New Orleans along the Arkansas River. In 1808, the Osage ceded eastern Oklahoma, north of the Arkansas River, to the United States. A decade later, the Quapaw relinquished lands south of that same river. The U.S. government bought the lands as territory for Native Americans it was intending to "remove" from the eastern United States to make way for westward-expanding white settlement. In 1817, U.S. government troops set up Fort Smith, in what would become the northeastern corner of Oklahoma. The troops were stationed there to keep peace between Native American groups who were fighting with each other.

## Displaced Peoples

In 1830, the U.S. Congress passed the Indian Removal Act. This act enabled the government to relocate Native people

......................................................................

▼ This nineteenth-century painting depicts Coronado and his men marching westward in 1541.

| Native Americans of Oklahoma by the late 1800s |
| --- |
| Apache |
| Arapaho |
| Caddo |
| Cherokee |
| Cheyenne |
| Chickasaw |
| Choctaw |
| Comanche |
| Creek |
| Delaware |
| Fox |
| Kansas |
| Kickapoo |
| Kiowa |
| Missouri |
| Modoc |
| Osage |
| Oto |
| Ottawa |
| Pawnee |
| Peoria |
| Ponca |
| Potawatomi |
| Quapaw |
| Sauk |
| Seminole |
| Tonkawa |
| Ute |
| Wichita |

from their lands in the southeastern United States to what became known as Indian Territory — eastern present-day Oklahoma. The five largest groups that were relocated — the Cherokee, Chickasaw, Choctaw, Creek, and Seminole — were known as the Five Civilized Tribes. Non-Native settlers had given them this name early in the 1800s because they had adopted some European or American customs, including large-scale farming and ownership of African slaves.

Native people did not leave willingly. The Creek and Seminole resisted violently, while the Cherokee sued the government. Their case came before the Supreme Court in 1832. In *Worcester v. Georgia*, Chief Justice John Marshall ruled that the Cherokee were a sovereign nation — the United States could not tell them what to do. The Court ruled that the Cherokee would have to agree to removal in a treaty that would then need to be ratified by Congress. Eventually, a tiny minority within the Cherokee nation agreed to sign a treaty, which President Andrew Jackson then used as justification for forcing them all west. In 1838, the U.S. Army began driving the Cherokee toward present-day Oklahoma, a trek later known as the Trail of Tears. Four thousand Cherokee died on the march.

Native groups who were already living in the Oklahoma region resented the government's relocation project. By 1837, the Kiowa and Comanche had signed treaties with the United

## The Five Civilized Tribes

Cherokee

Chickasaw

Choctaw

Creek

Seminole

▼ This painting by Robert Lindneux shows the tragic 1830s relocation of Native Americans to Oklahoma. The artwork is on exhibit at the Woolaroc Museum near Bartlesville.

States, allowing the government to move eastern tribes through their area into the western part of the territory. After 1840, however, the Kiowa, Comanche, Cheyenne, and Apache joined forces to fight the intrusion of the newcomers. They also fought with U.S. troops who protected the new immigrants, until the Treaty of Medicine Lodge was signed in 1867.

## Indian Territory and the Native American Nations

In 1851, the U.S. district court for the Western District of Arkansas was established at Fort Smith, Arkansas. This court oversaw all legal cases in Indian Territory and became the headquarters for U.S. policy toward Native Americans in the Southwest.

In Indian Territory, each group formed its own nation. The U.S. government signed treaties promising to protect these nations and their new lands "as long as grass shall grow and rivers run." Most of these Native American communities were located in eastern Oklahoma. Because of the treaties between the Five Civilized Tribes and the U.S. government, the flow of settlers westward did not have any immediate effect on Oklahoma's new Native American residents.

## The Civil War

In 1861, tensions over whether slavery should be allowed in the United States flared into war. Southern states left the Union and formed the Confederate States of America. Oklahoma did not join either side, and no major battles of the war were fought in the area, although local fighting did take place. Most members of the Five Civilized Tribes sided with the Confederacy. Others fought for the Union, and still others did not take sides at all. After the Civil War, the U.S. government punished the Five Civilized Tribes

# Buffalo Soldiers in the Sooner State

In contrast to their counterparts in most other states, African Americans had many career opportunities in the Oklahoma region during the Civil War period.

They worked the land as farmers, drove cattle as cowboys, and homesteaded just as the white settlers did. Many African Americans fought in the Union Army during the Civil War and were instrumental in the Union victory over Confederate forces.

Following the conclusion of the Civil War, the U.S. Congress created the Ninth and Tenth Cavalry regiments, permanent African-American military units based at Fort Gibson and Fort Sill. These soldiers were dubbed "Buffalo Soldiers" by the local Native Americans, because they fought with the ferocity and courage of the buffalo.

for siding with the Confederacy by taking away land it had given them in the western part of Indian Territory. The government then began relocating other eastern tribes, such as the Delaware and other Plains tribes, to the land it had confiscated.

In the late 1860s, Texas ranchers drove millions of cattle across Indian Territory on their way to the railroad hubs of Kansas. For the rights to use these lands, a group of cattle ranchers signed a five-year lease in 1883 for more than 6 million acres (2.4 million hectares) of Indian Territory. The agreement was contrary to federal law, however, and it was declared invalid. In 1890, President Benjamin Harrison ordered the cattlemen to remove their animals from Indian Territory.

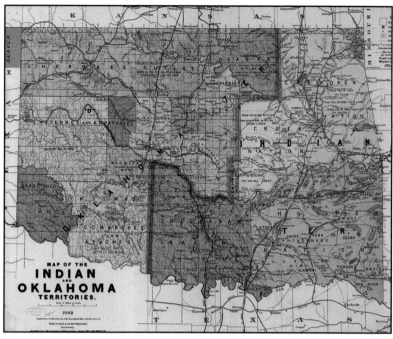

▲ This 1892 map shows the outline of what was Indian Territory (*east of red line*) and the Oklahoma Territory (*west of red line*) before the state of Oklahoma was created.

## Boomers and Sooners

Oklahoma's "Unassigned Lands" were so named because no Native people had been forced onto them. These areas included segments at the center of the modern state, Greer County to the southwest, and the Panhandle. There were small pockets of white settlement, but, for the most part, the Unassigned Lands were not open to homesteading. In 1879, a group known as the "Boomers" began pressuring the federal government to allow non-Native settlers into these areas.

The government finally agreed, and it bought more than 3 million acres (1.2 million ha) of Creek and Seminole land to open up the pockets of Unassigned Lands. On April 22, 1889, the government gave nearly 1.9 million acres (769,000 ha) to settlers by means of a "land run." A government official fired a pistol into the air, and thousands of prospective settlers —

▼ The city of Guthrie as it appeared in 1910. On April 21, 1889, Guthrie did not exist. Thanks to a land run, by the next evening it was a city of ten thousand people.

until then held back by the U.S. Army — were allowed to ride or run into Oklahoma to stake the claims on which they would soon build their farms and homes.

Approximately fifty thousand legal settlers entered Oklahoma that first day. Cities of ten thousand people, including Guthrie and Oklahoma City, appeared overnight. Those who entered illegally, before the official opening date, came to be known as "Sooners." Both the land-run method and lotteries were later used to establish claims elsewhere in Oklahoma.

## The Road to Statehood

On May 2, 1890, the Unassigned Lands officially became the Oklahoma Territory, and the Panhandle was also formally added to Oklahoma. George W. Steele was appointed the territory's first governor, and Guthrie became its capital. Maps made after 1890 split the Oklahoma region into Indian Territory and the Oklahoma Territory, together known as the Twin Territories. Indian Territory was all the land then controlled by the Five Civilized Tribes and other Native American nations, while the Oklahoma Territory was where non-Native settlers lived. The settlers soon began demanding that the federal government let them settle in Indian Territory.

Congress established the Dawes Commission, which began land negotiations with the Five Civilized Tribes. The Dawes Commission persuaded the Native American nations to disband their tribal governments, incorporate their towns, become U.S. citizens, and allow their individual members to assume land ownership. A process of government land allotment began on April 1, 1899. All lands not allotted to individual tribe members were made available to non-Native settlers, either by land run or lottery.

In 1905, the people of Indian Territory (80 percent of whom were non-Native) proposed the creation of a new state called Sequoyah. The U.S. Congress rejected this effort, and the Indian and Oklahoma Territories were combined into the single state of Oklahoma. It became

## Cowmen and Plowmen

**D**uring the 1880s, the Oklahoma region's main economic strength came from both farms and ranches covered by vast herds of longhorn cattle. Farmers and ranchers frequently came into conflict during these years, because the farmers tended to fence off lands that the ranchers needed to cross in order to drive their herds to the big-city livestock markets. Fortunately, by 1890 railroad transportation had made large-scale cattle drives — and the so-called "range wars" between the farmers and ranchers — unnecessary. This conflict between farmers and cowboys, as well as its eventual peaceful resolution, was immortalized in the musical *Oklahoma!* In a song called "The Farmer and the Cowman," a chorus of Sooners sings that the two warring groups "should be friends."

the Union's forty-sixth state on November 16, 1907. Guthrie was the capital, and Charles Haskell was elected as the new state's first governor.

## The Twentieth Century

Oklahoma's oil production began in 1897 with a large well at Bartlesville. During U.S. involvement in World War I, demand soared for the products of Oklahoma's farms and oil fields. Unfortunately, farm prices plunged during the 1920s, causing mass unemployment and social upheaval. The Ku Klux Klan and other racist organizations blamed the hard economic times on Oklahoma's minorities and killed many innocent people in lynchings. The Klan developed a strong influence over public opinion and the state's elected officials. Governor James B. A. Robertson, who served from 1919 to 1923, opposed the Klan, however, and prohibited all state officials from joining the organization.

In 1921, African Americans in Tulsa held an anti-lynching rally. The rally sparked a riot, during which some three hundred African Americans died and thirty-five city blocks were destroyed. (Oklahoma's unjust segregation laws were finally overturned in 1964, thanks in no small part to the peaceful protests organized by Clara Luper and other African-American Civil Rights activists in Oklahoma.)

Oklahoma made it through the rough times of the 1920s in part because of the discovery of large oil and gas deposits. Oklahoma City's enormous oil field began producing in 1928, and within a decade the field had more than fifteen hundred productive wells. Oklahoma's Greater Seminole Oil Field, in the southeastern part of the state, became the nation's oil leader during the late 1920s.

▼ Thousands of refugees from the Dust Bowl conditions of Oklahoma headed west in the 1930s. This family, photographed in 1936, made it all the way to California.

## The Dirty '30s

The Great Depression, which began in 1929, brought economic grief to Oklahoma. Both the oil business and agriculture suffered from declining prices. Banks failed across the state, wiping out the life savings of many families. Drought conditions devastated crops from 1932 to 1937, and severe winds stripped away topsoil, creating dust storms that blotted out the sun. Vast areas of the Great Plains — including Oklahoma — became known as the Dust Bowl. Thousands of people fled Oklahoma during the 1930s, causing a significant drop in the state's population. Many of these migrants, known as Okies, set out for California.

## World War II and Postwar Expansion

Because of the wartime demand for fuels and farm products, Oklahoma's economy recovered quickly once the United States entered World War II in 1941. Many farmers who had been hard hit during the preceding Dust Bowl years salvaged their lands through new soil conservation techniques.

The 1950s brought change to Oklahoma's economy, which began shifting away from agriculture and even further toward oil production and other heavy industries. Farms diminished in both size and number during the 1950s and 1960s. Also, Oklahoma City became the home of a training and research center for the Federal Aviation Administration.

The 1960s and 1970s saw the completion of several dams and artificial lakes, which increased Oklahoma's water supplies and provided hydroelectric power as well. The McClellan-Kerr Arkansas River Navigation System was completed in 1970, enabling Oklahoma's goods to reach markets via the Mississippi River. From 1976 to 1980, the state's oil and natural gas producers also benefited greatly from a growing worldwide demand for energy. By the mid-1990s, Oklahoma seemed to be on track to a bright future. Then disaster struck.

On April 19, 1995, a truck bomb exploded in front of the Alfred P. Murrah Federal Building in Oklahoma City. The bomb, made by a domestic terrorist, killed 168 people and injured more than 500. Oklahomans rallied around the city and quickly built a beautiful memorial to the victims. Since that time, the state's future has indeed been looking brighter, as oil prices rise and urban development brings renewed prosperity to the downtown area of Oklahoma City.

▲ The Oklahoma City National Memorial honors those lost in the 1995 explosion.

### Rising from the Ashes

**W**ords on the Oklahoma City National Memorial read: "We come here to remember those who were killed, those who survived and those changed forever. May all who leave here know the impact of violence. May this memorial offer comfort, strength, peace, hope, and serenity."

# Just Plain Folks

> My ancestors didn't come over on the Mayflower,
> but they met 'em at the boat.
>
> — *Will Rogers, humorist and actor from Oklahoma*

Despite its size, Oklahoma contains relatively few people. Oklahoma's current population density is 50.3 people per square mile (19.4 people per sq km), considerably less than the national figure of 79.6 people per square mile (30.7 per sq km).

Between 1990 and 2000, the state's population increased by 9.7 percent, which is less than the national average of 13.1 percent, but double the rate of increase from 1980 to 1990. The principal reason for Oklahoma's strong population growth is the steady diversification of the state's economy beyond the traditional oil, mining, and agricultural sectors. Jobs in the manufacture of high-technology goods have encouraged newcomers to settle in the Sooner State. Women make up a slightly larger portion — 50.9 percent — of the state's population than men do. The median age in the state is 35.5.

## Age Distribution in Oklahoma
### (2000 Census)

| | |
|---|---|
| 0–4 | 236,353 |
| 5–19 | 765,927 |
| 20–24 | 247,165 |
| 25–44 | 975,169 |
| 45–64 | 770,090 |
| 65 & over | 455,950 |

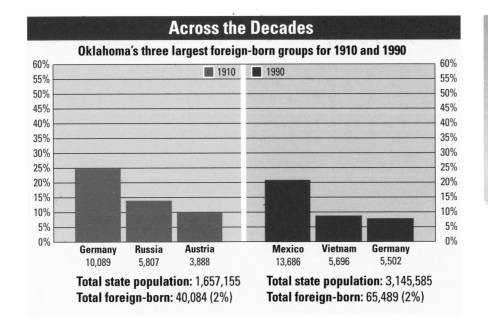

## Across the Decades

### Oklahoma's three largest foreign-born groups for 1910 and 1990

■ 1910    ■ 1990

| Germany | Russia | Austria | Mexico | Vietnam | Germany |
|---|---|---|---|---|---|
| 10,089 | 5,807 | 3,888 | 13,686 | 5,696 | 5,502 |

**Total state population: 1,657,155**
**Total foreign-born: 40,084 (2%)**

**Total state population: 3,145,585**
**Total foreign-born: 65,489 (2%)**

## Patterns of Immigration

The total number of people who immigrated to Oklahoma in 1999 was 2,376. Of that number, the largest immigrant groups were from Mexico (33%), Vietnam (12%), and India (8%).

## Immigration

The growth of Oklahoma's population once proceeded at a much quicker pace than it does today. The land rushes of the 1880s brought stampedes of settlers into the region. Northern Oklahoma tended to attract people from Midwestern states such as Kansas, while southerners from Arkansas and Texas homesteaded the areas south of the Canadian River. These settlers had English, Irish, Scottish, and German roots. Settlers also came to Oklahoma directly from western and eastern Europe during the nineteenth century. Today, the descendants of these settlers make up the majority of the population.

Native Americans and Alaska Natives make up Oklahoma's largest minority group, at 7.9 percent of the population, a figure far higher than the national average of 0.9 percent. Oklahoma is home to more than sixty tribes and thirty-nine tribal governments.

▲ This 1909 photograph shows a group of Cheyenne gathered in Oklahoma for a powwow, at which the traditional sun dance was performed.

## Heritage and Background, Oklahoma                    Year 2000

► Here's a look at the racial backgrounds of Oklahomans today. Oklahoma ranks twenty-fourth among all U.S. states with regard to African Americans as a percentage of the population.

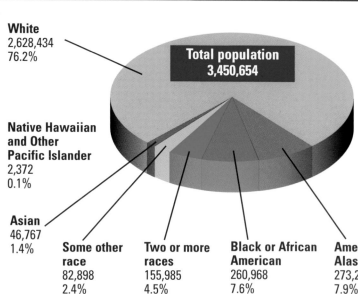

**Total population 3,450,654**

White
2,628,434
76.2%

Native Hawaiian and Other Pacific Islander
2,372
0.1%

Asian
46,767
1.4%

Some other race
82,898
2.4%

Two or more races
155,985
4.5%

Black or African American
260,968
7.6%

American Indian and Alaska Native
273,230
7.9%

**Note:** 5.2% (179,304) of the population identify themselves as **Hispanic** or **Latino,** a cultural designation that crosses racial lines. Hispanics and Latinos are counted in this category as well as the racial category of their choice.

## Where Do Oklahomans Live?

Throughout most of Oklahoma's history, people have lived mainly in rural areas. Because of the economic shifts of the mid-twentieth century, however, the population has become increasingly urbanized. Although only a few more than half a million people live within the boundaries of Oklahoma City, about one million live in the greater metropolitan area that surrounds and includes the city. This means that almost one-third of the people in the state live in or around their capital.

Oklahoma's Native American populations are distributed throughout the state, but large concentrations can be found in the big cities, on the sprawling Osage Reservation lands of northeastern Oklahoma, and in towns such as Okmulgee, the site of a Creek cultural center. The Sooner State's African-American population is most highly concentrated in Oklahoma City. Oklahoma also boasts more than two dozen small towns established by former African-American slaves, who were freed after the Civil War.

## Education

More than six hundred thousand Oklahomans attend public schools in the state, and, as of 1999, Oklahoma spends more than $3.5 billion on public education, which breaks down to $5,684 per pupil.

▼ Oklahoma City offers a pleasant combination of residential neighborhoods and a dynamic downtown district.

The state of Oklahoma gives financial support to a university system, including Northeastern State University in Tahlequah, Northwestern Oklahoma State University in Alvar, Oklahoma State University in Stillwater, Southeastern Oklahoma State University in Durant, Southwestern Oklahoma State University in Weatherford, and the University of Oklahoma in Norman. More than a dozen privately funded colleges and universities also flourish in the Sooner State. The federal government operates two boarding schools in Oklahoma, institutions designed to cater to the needs of Native American children.

## Religion

The majority of Oklahomans — approximately 86 percent — belong to various Christian denominations, with Southern Baptists and Methodists predominating. Some 33 percent of Oklahomans are Baptists, around 10 percent are Methodists, and upward of 8 percent are Catholics. Presbyterians make up about 1 percent, as do Episcopalians. Followers of Native American religions account for less than 1 percent of the population, although Oklahoma's Native American population is nearly eight times this figure. Jews, Buddhists, and Hindus together represent less than 2 percent of the total population. Around 6.5 percent of Oklahomans identify themselves as nonreligious.

**DID YOU KNOW?**

Oklahoma City covers one of the largest land areas of any city in the United States. It extends over an area of 607 sq miles (1,572 sq km). New York City, with sixteen times the population, has only half this area.

| Educational Levels of Oklahoma Workers (age 25 and over) | |
| --- | --- |
| Less than 9th grade | 195,015 |
| 9th to 12th grade, no diploma | 311,946 |
| High school graduate, including equivalency | 607,903 |
| Some college, no degree or associate degree | 525,591 |
| Bachelor's degree | 236,112 |
| Graduate or professional degree | 118,857 |

# The Lay of the Land

All the sounds of the earth are like music,
The breeze is so busy, it don't miss a tree,
And a ol' weepin' willer is laughin' at me.
Oh, what a beautiful mornin',
Oh, what a beautiful day.
— *from "Oh, What a Beautiful Mornin'," from* Oklahoma!
*by Richard Rodgers and Oscar Hammerstein II*

Oklahoma covers several of North America's key physiographic features. The most prominent are the limestone- and shale-rich Ozark Plateau of the northeast; the steep Ouachita Mountains of the southeast; the Arbuckle Mountains of the south-central region; the Wichita Mountains of the southwest; the Gypsum Hills that run from north to south across the state's western region; the Red Beds Plains and Sandstone Hills of central Oklahoma; and the High Plains of the Panhandle in the northwest. The Panhandle is part of the Great Plains, lands that supported dozens of Native American groups, as well as enormous buffalo herds, for many centuries before European settlement.

## Resources

Oklahoma is a treasure trove of mineral wealth. The first discovery of petroleum was in 1859; five decades later, Oklahoma had taken its place as one of the nation's leading oil producers. The eastern part of the state also contains

**Highest Point**
**Black Mesa**
4,973 feet (1,516 m) above sea level

▼ *From left to right:* wild verbena; Natural Falls State Park; wild sunflowers; a red fox; Tucker Tower on Lake Murray; Wichita Mountains Wildlife Refuge.

extensive deposits of coal, as well as dolomite, granite, gypsum, lead, limestone, and salt. Hydroelectric dams, mainly on the Arkansas River system, now provide a small percentage of Oklahoma's electrical power. The Sooner State's wide plains are topped with fertile soils that support wheat fields, grazing pastures for cattle, and forests.

## Climate

Oklahoma's climate is generally warm and dry, although it varies from one region to another. Weather conditions in northwestern Oklahoma, where elevations are higher, tend to be cooler and drier than in the warmer, more humid southeast. In the southeast, the growing season lasts 238 days, on average; the drier, cooler Panhandle has about 168 days of agricultural growth. Situated on the edge of an arid zone, portions of western Oklahoma are subject to periodic droughts. During droughts in the Dust Bowl years of the 1930s, much of the region's fertile topsoil was lost to wind erosion. Tornadoes are common in Oklahoma. In 1999, more than a dozen tornadoes touched down in the center of the state in one day. The tornadoes killed forty-two people in Oklahoma and Kansas.

## Lakes and Rivers

Approximately one hundred small natural lakes exist in Oklahoma, and river dams have created more than twice that many artificial ones. The largest of these artificial lakes is the Eufaula Lake in east-central Oklahoma, which offers boating and fishing activities. One of Oklahoma's other important large lakes is Lake Texoma, a popular recreational destination that gets its name from the fact that it lies partly in Texas and partly in Oklahoma.

All the excess rain, snow, and other precipitation that falls on Oklahoma drains into the Gulf of Mexico via two

**Average January temperature**
Lawton: 44°F (6.7°C)
Tulsa: 35.2°F (1.8°C)

**Average July temperature**
Lawton: 81°F (27.2°C)
Tulsa: 83.2°F (28.4°C)

**Average yearly rainfall**
Lawton: 28.0 inches (71.1 cm)
Tulsa: 38.8 inches (98.6 cm)

**Average yearly snowfall**
Lawton: 8.0 inches (20.3 cm)
Tulsa: 9.0 inches (22.9 cm)

### Largest Lakes

**Eufaula Reservoir (Eufaula Lake)**
105,600 acres (42,736 ha)

**Lake Texoma**
90,880 acres (36,779 ha)

**Grand Lake O' the Cherokees**
46,500 acres (18,819 ha)

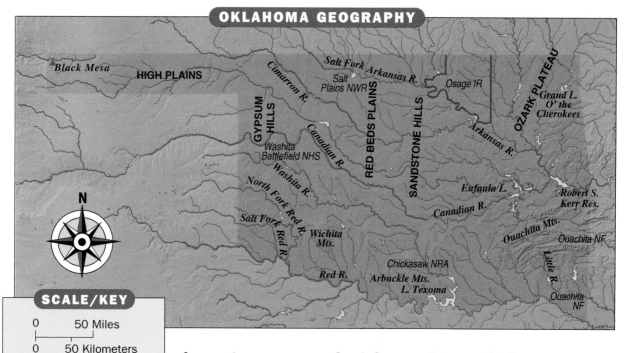

**SCALE/KEY**

| 0 | 50 Miles |
|---|---|
| 0 | 50 Kilometers |

| IR | Indian Reservation |
|---|---|
| NF | National Forest |
| NHS | National Historic Site |
| NRA | National Recreation Area |
| NWR | National Wildlife Refuge |
| ▲ | Highest Point |
| | Mountains |

### Major Rivers

**Arkansas River**
1,459 miles (2,348 km)

**Red River**
1,290 miles (2,076 km)

**Canadian River**
906 miles (1,458 km)

large river systems: the Arkansas River, which crosses the northeastern part of the state; and the Red River, which forms the border with Oklahoma's southern neighbor, Texas. Both of these river systems support shipping traffic. Among the major rivers that flow into the Arkansas River are the Canadian, Chikaskia, and Cimarron Rivers.

## Plants and Animals

The most common vegetation on Oklahoma's plains are grasses. Wide central and southwesterly areas of the state support savanna and tall grasses such as bluestem, Indian grass, and sand grass, while the northwestern regions tend to be covered in bunchgrasses and short grasses such as wire grass, buffalo grass, and grama. These grasses help sustain millions of head of Oklahoma cattle. The plains are also home to black-eyed Susans, butterfly weeds, cacti, mesquites, prairie coneflowers, and sagebrush. Just about every region of the state is home to anemones, goldenrods, sunflowers, verbenas, violets, and indigos.

About 20 percent of Oklahoma's area is forestland, containing more than 130 varieties of trees, including ash, cedar, cottonwood, cypress, dogwood, elm, hickory, pecan, pine, sweet gum, and walnut. Blackjack oak and post oak trees are common in central Oklahoma's Cross Timbers region. The northeast's Ozark Plateau maintains a profusion of oak and hickory forests, while oak and pine abound in the southeasterly Ouachita Mountains. Oklahoma's principal commercial forests lie in the east and southeast.

The state's plains support an abundance of small animals, including armadillos, prairie dogs, and rabbits, as well as coyotes. The state's forest habitats nurture antelope, deer, elk, gray foxes, red foxes, minks, opossums, raccoons, and fox and gray squirrels. The Wichita Mountains Wildlife Refuge, located near the city of Lawton, is home to small herds of buffalo as well as deer, moose, and Texas longhorn cattle. Among Oklahoma's most common birds are blue jays, cardinals, hawks, sparrows, meadowlarks, and scissor-tailed flycatchers. The scissor-tail was once hunted for its long tail feathers, which were used as hat decorations. Every October, about ten million crows come to roost at the Fort Cobb Recreation Area near Anadarko. Ducks and geese frequently visit the state as well.

Oklahoma's rivers and lakes allow fish such as bass, buffalofish, carp, catfish, drumfish, paddlefish, and sunfish to thrive. Among the Sooner State's many national wildlife refuges are the Chickasaw National Recreation Area, the Salt Plains National Wildlife Refuge, and the Ouachita National Forest. The habitat of Oklahoma's plants and animals is protected in such places, while still allowing humans to enjoy the natural bounty of the Sooner State.

▼ American white pelicans are seasonal visitors at the Salt Plains National Wildlife Refuge.

# Oil, Soil, and Toil

> [Oklahoma] is the aroma of rich crude oil fused with the scent of sweat and sacred smoke.
> — *Michael Wallis, writer,*
> Way Down Yonder in the Indian Nation, *1993*

During territorial times, rich soils, abundant water, and a benign climate became the first engines to power Oklahoma's economy. Toward the end of the nineteenth century, the discovery of the region's vast deposits of petroleum added greatly to Oklahoma's wealth. Oklahoma has turned out to have some of the nation's largest oil reserves. Significant quantities of oil and natural gas have been found in virtually every county in the state. The central region (encompassing Oklahoma City) leads the state in oil production, while the western region contains the highest natural gas concentrations. More than 60 percent of Oklahoma's natural gas is sent into other states through pipelines.

Oklahoma City's vast oil fields were discovered in 1928 and have been developed extensively ever since. Oklahoma also has significant coal-mining operations, especially in LeFlore County and other east-central and northeasterly areas. Coal-burning facilities generate about 60 percent of the state's electricity, while about 33 percent is produced from natural gas. The remainder comes from hydroelectric dams, many on the Arkansas River system.

## Agriculture

Today, some 75 percent of Oklahoma's lands are devoted to agriculture, with about 86,000 farms and ranches currently in operation, covering 34 million acres (13.76 million ha) of land. The state's more than five million beef cattle provide the largest incomes for the agricultural sector. Chickens, eggs, hogs, and hatchery catfish also provide significant livestock revenue.

| Top Employers (of workers age sixteen and over.) |
|---|
| Services . . . . . . . 32.5% |
| Wholesale and retail trade . . . . . 21.5% |
| Manufacturing . . 14.2% |
| Transportation, communications, public utilities . . . 7.4% |
| Public Administration . . . 6.3% |
| Finance, insurance, and real estate . . . . . . 5.7% |
| Construction . . . . 5.5% |
| Agriculture, forestry, and fisheries . . . . . . . . 3.7% |
| Mining . . . . . . . . . 3.1% |

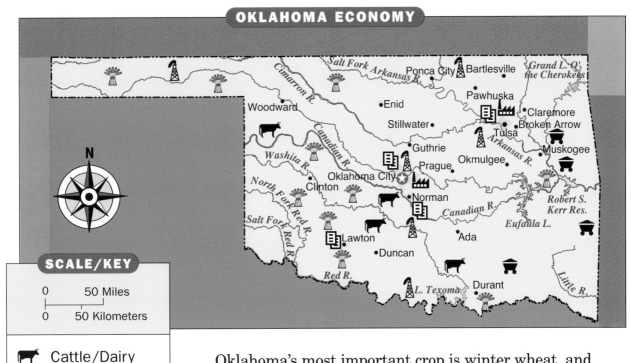

0    50 Miles

0    50 Kilometers

- 🐂 Cattle/Dairy
- 🌾 Farming
- 🏭 Manufacturing
- 🛒 Mining
- ⛽ Oil/Natural Gas
- 🏢 Services
- Urban Areas

Oklahoma's most important crop is winter wheat, and the state is one of the nation's biggest wheat producers. The Sooner State's next most important cash crop is hay, followed by products such as cotton, corn, and sorghum. Oklahoma's farmers were particularly hard hit by the farm slumps of the 1970s and 1980s, with some three thousand farms either going out of business or being sold between 1985 and 1987. Subsidies, which are funds given to farmers by the U.S. government, have helped agriculture recover. The consolidation of smaller farms into larger units has also helped to make agriculture more profitable.

## Oklahoma Gross State Product

**Millions of dollars**

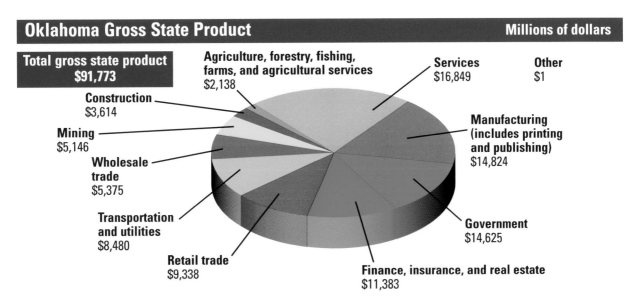

Total gross state product
**$91,773**

Agriculture, forestry, fishing, farms, and agricultural services
$2,138

Services
$16,849

Other
$1

Construction
$3,614

Mining
$5,146

Wholesale trade
$5,375

Transportation and utilities
$8,480

Retail trade
$9,338

Manufacturing (includes printing and publishing)
$14,824

Government
$14,625

Finance, insurance, and real estate
$11,383

## Manufacturing

Oklahoma's abundant energy and labor have made the state attractive to many manufacturing industries during recent decades. Most of the state's manufacturing enterprises are centered in a narrow region that extends from Oklahoma City northeast to the border with Missouri. Some of Oklahoma's most important manufactured goods are electronics and computer equipment, made mostly in Oklahoma City and Tulsa, and machinery for use by the oil and construction industries.

## Service Industries and Transportation

Service industries make up a large percentage of the Sooner State's annual gross state product (the total value of a state's goods and services) and employ more Oklahomans than any other economic activity. These service industries are clustered in urban areas such as Oklahoma City, Tulsa, and Norman.

Tulsa and Oklahoma City serve as the state's leading financial centers. Transportation, communications, and utilities are other important elements of the economy. The fuel industry relies upon trucking companies and some 5,000 miles (8,045 km) of pipelines to move its products to utility companies and consumers.

The Missouri-Kansas-Texas Railroad crossed Oklahoma by 1872 and provided a critical outlet for the territory's farm products. Over the next half-century, however, the large-scale construction of roads gradually diminished the

### Made in Oklahoma

**Leading farm products and crops**
Beef cattle
Broiler chickens
Wheat
Hay
Cotton
Corn
Sorghum
Dairy products
Eggs
Hogs
Hatchery catfish

**Other products**
Electrical equipment
Fabricated metal products
Gypsum
Machinery
Natural gas
Petroleum

economic importance of the railroads. The Sooner State now boasts approximately 112,000 miles (180,200 km) of roads, freeways, and toll highways, including the Turner Turnpike, a toll highway that connects Oklahoma City with Tulsa. Oklahoma City and Tulsa both have bustling international airports. This increasing ease of transportation has not only boosted Oklahoma's trade revenues; it has also nurtured a growing tourist industry.

## Recent Economic Developments

Oklahoma's economy has shifted greatly since the middle of the last century, moving away from its traditional strong reliance on agriculture. Oklahoma's oil industry, coupled with the state's assorted service industries, dwarfs the farm sector. The rise of the oil industry, however, has not been without its problems during recent years. The economic slumps of the 1980s, which devastated the Sooner State's farmers, also caused a worldwide decline in fuel prices, hitting the energy sector hard. During the late 1990s, Oklahoma's energy prospects brightened as world oil demand — and prices — climbed.

| Major Airports | | |
|---|---|---|
| Airport | Location | Passengers per year (2000) |
| Tulsa International Airport | Tulsa | 3,482,814 |
| Will Rogers World Airport | Oklahoma City | 3,481,789 |

▼ An oil field near Enid in 1917, during the state's first oil boom.

# Oklahoma Order

It's a good thing we don't get all the
government we pay for.

— *Will Rogers, humorist*

I n 1905, the leadership of Indian Territory's Five Civilized Tribes met at Muskogee to discuss statehood, and they invited the region's non-Native majority to take part. Their plan was to convince the U.S. Congress to admit the territory as the state of Sequoyah, an idea that had already received local voter approval. Although the convention adopted a constitution, Congress wasn't interested in admitting Sequoyah; it preferred to bring the Twin Territories (Indian Territory and the Oklahoma Territory) into the Union together as a single state, which we now call Oklahoma. The following year, territorial delegates met to draft a new constitution, and President Theodore Roosevelt officially approved Oklahoma's statehood application on November 16, 1907.

The Sooner State still operates under its original 1907 constitution, although the document has been amended a number of times since then. Constitutional amendments may be initiated either by the state legislature or by means of voter petitions. The legislature has the authority to call a constitutional convention to redraft the document, so long as the voters approve. Because of the Oklahoma constitution's initiative and referendum sections, voters are empowered to propose laws and vote on them without action by the legislature.

## State Constitution

**A**ll political power is inherent in the people; and government is instituted for their protection, security, and benefit, and to promote their general welfare; and they have the right to alter or reform the same whenever the public good may require it: Provided, such change be not repugnant to the Constitution of the United States.

— *from Section 11-1 of the Oklahoma Constitution, 1907*

## Executive Branch

Oklahoma's chief executive officer is the governor, who is elected to serve a four-year term. The governor may serve no more than two consecutive terms but may run again after four years out of office. The governor is in charge of appointing several other executive-branch officers, including the secretary of state and the heads of the various

## Elected Posts in the Executive Branch

| Office | Length of Term | Term Limits |
|---|---|---|
| Governor | 4 years | 2 terms |
| Lieutenant Governor | 4 years | None |
| Attorney General | 4 years | None |
| Treasurer | 4 years | None |
| Auditor and Inspector | 4 years | None |
| Superintendent of Public Instruction | 4 years | None |
| Insurance Commissioner | 4 years | None |
| Labor Commissioner | 4 years | None |
| Corporation Commissioners | 4 years | None |

state budget and revenue departments and agencies, although certain department leaders are selected by special commissions. Oklahoma's other elected executive positions are lieutenant governor, attorney general, treasurer, auditor and inspector, superintendent of public instruction, insurance commissioner, labor commissioner, and corporation commissioners. All of them serve terms of four years.

## Legislative Branch

Oklahoma's state lawmaking body is known as the Oklahoma Legislature. It is composed of a 48-member senate and a 101-member house of representatives. Voters elect each legislator from their respective senate and house districts across the state. Senate members serve four-year terms, while representatives serve two-year terms. In 1990, Oklahoma's voters limited the number of years legislators may remain in office to a cumulative total of twelve. The legislature meets annually, beginning on the first Monday in February. In odd-numbered years, it also meets for an extra day to allow the lawmakers some additional time to examine and verify the results of public elections.

## Judicial Branch

The highest court in Oklahoma is the supreme court, which ultimately settles all cases from lower courts when the outcomes are under appeal (dispute). The

▼ The oil well that stands next to the Oklahoma state capitol is named "Petunia," because drilling first began in the middle of a flower bed.

Oklahoma Supreme Court consists of nine justices, who are appointed by the governor based upon the recommendations of a judicial nominating commission. During the first general election after entering office, each new supreme court justice must run in a nonpartisan election in order to qualify for the right to remain in office for the remainder of an initial six-year term. Justices who lose these elections are turned out of office before completing their terms. The nine justices select one of their own number to lead the court as its chief justice. Oklahoma's judicial branch also maintains a court of criminal appeals, which is presided over by twelve or more judges. The selection process for these judges is handled in the same manner as with the supreme court. Less urgent cases are handled by district and county courts, where judges are elected to four-year terms.

## Local Government

Each of Oklahoma's seventy-seven counties is run by a trio of county commissioners, elected from separate districts. The state's approximately 590 incorporated towns and cities, as well as its hundreds of smaller, unincorporated areas, have a variety of governmental options. Cities with two thousand or more residents may adopt their own administrative charters and can amend them when necessary. Most cities use either a mayor and city council or a city council and city manager form of local government. Oklahoma's Legislature has divided the state into eleven planning districts to increase the efficiency and coordination of various state functions, including law enforcement, economic development, health, and community planning. These districts help integrate the efforts of local officials with various state and federal agencies.

## Party Politics

The Sooner State has long been a stronghold of the Democratic party, and most Oklahomans are registered Democrats today. For more than half a century after

### The Original Sooner Capital

**A**lthough Oklahoma City has served as Oklahoma's state capital since 1910 (just three years after the state entered the Union), the land-rush town of Guthrie held that honor during the territorial period, beginning in 1890. After the capital moved permanently to Oklahoma City, new construction in downtown Guthrie — as well as the demolition of old buildings — came to a virtual halt. Today, about one hundred of the original nineteenth-century buildings in downtown Guthrie are considered monuments and are preserved and protected by the National Register of Historic Places. Thanks to restoration efforts undertaken during the 1980s, about 90 percent of Guthrie's downtown area now stands as a living museum of the architecture and history of Oklahoma's pre-statehood past.

| Legislature | | | |
|---|---|---|---|
| House | Number of Members | Length of Term | Term Limits |
| Senate | 48 senators | 4 years | 3 terms* |
| House of Representatives | 101 representatives | 2 years | 6 terms* |

* Legislators may serve no more than twelve years in a lifetime.

Oklahoma achieved statehood, only Democrats served as governors. By the 1960s, however, the Republican party had become increasingly influential. In 1963, the party finally succeeded in taking the governor's mansion, when Henry Bellmon was sworn in as Oklahoma's eighteenth governor. Despite the state's preference for Democratic presidents, Republicans are now as likely as Democrats to win Oklahoma's gubernatorial elections, as well as its state legislative or U.S. Senate seats.

## Tribal Government

The Cherokee Nation has its headquarters in Tahlequah and operates as a sovereign government with the ability to raise taxes and make laws. A principal chief and deputy chief are elected to four-year terms by registered Cherokee voters and serve as the executive officers of the nation. The legislative branch of the government consists of a fifteen-member tribal council, with the deputy chief as its head. The Cherokee Nation has a judicial system that includes district courts and the judicial appeals tribunal, which is the highest court.

▼ The Logan County Courthouse in Guthrie served as the seat of state government from 1907 until 1910, when the state capital was moved to Oklahoma City.

# Have a Ball

> I'm proud to be an Okie from Muskogee,
> A place where even squares can have a ball
> — *from "An Okie from Muskogee"*
> *by Merle Haggard, 1969*

Oklahomans enjoy a vibrant tradition of live classical and popular music as well as theater and dance. Oklahoma City and Tulsa each supports its own symphony as well as theater and dance companies. Privately funded theater companies also thrive in cities such as Clinton, Enid, and Muskogee. The annual OKMOZART Festival at Bartlesville attracts world-class performers and large, enthusiastic audiences, while the smaller cities of Durant and Edmond are known for their summer Shakespeare productions.

One of Oklahoma's most renowned musical sons is folk singer and composer Woody Guthrie, whose songs illuminated the working man's economic and political struggles during the Depression years. Many modern-day stars of popular music are Sooners, including Garth Brooks, Vince Gill, and Reba McEntire.

Oklahoma's contributions to the field of dance include the famous Native American ballerinas Maria and Marjorie Tallchief, Yvonne Chouteau, Rosella Hightower, and Moscelyne Larkin. World-class opera singers David Pittman-Jennings, Chris Merritt, and Leona Mitchell all began their careers in Oklahoma.

## Painting, Sculpture, and the Graphic Arts

One of the best-known artists to hail from Oklahoma is Charles Banks Wilson, whose four famous murals depicting scenes from the Sooner State's history adorn the dome of Oklahoma City's capitol. The murals each measure 13 feet (4 m) tall and approximately 26 feet (8 m) wide and are based on Wilson's meticulous historical research. Award-

### Steinbeck's Stark Vision

The Dust Bowl years of the 1930s did more than devastate Oklahoma's farmlands, families, and economy — it also inspired a great novel. In 1939, while the entire nation suffered in the grip of the Great Depression, John Steinbeck published *The Grapes of Wrath,* a brutally honest depiction of the plight of a family of Okies, or Oklahomans who fled the Dust Bowl to seek their fortunes in California.

In 1940, Steinbeck's novel won the Pulitzer Prize and was made into a movie by director John Ford.

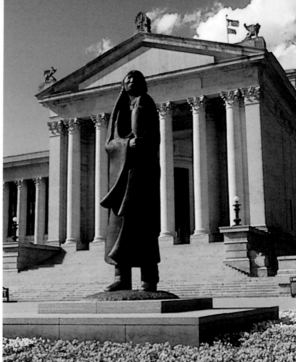

winning Chiricahua Apache sculptor Allan Houser is another important Oklahoma artist. His statue of a proud Native American, titled *As Long as the Waters Flow,* stands outside Oklahoma's capitol.

Oklahoma City hosts two important art exhibits each June: the Prix de West Invitational Sale and Exhibition, and the Red Earth Native American Cultural Festival. The Oklahoma State Arts Council also runs an Artists-in-Residence program, through which young people can take classes taught by professional artists.

## Oklahoma: Page, Stage, and Screen

The Sooner State's colorful history has moved generations of creative people. John Steinbeck's 1939 novel, *The Grapes of Wrath,* won the Pulitzer Prize for literature for its incisive portrayal of the plight of a family of "Okies," who fled the devastation of northwest Oklahoma's Dust Bowl during the 1930s. Wesley Ruggles's 1931 film *Cimarron* (based on Edna Ferber's novel of the same name) was set against the backdrop of Oklahoma's heady land-rush days and became the first Western-genre film to win the Academy Award for Best Picture. That same year, Lynn Riggs's play *Green Grow the Lilacs* debuted; a dozen years later, Richard Rodgers and Oscar Hammerstein II adapted it to the Broadway stage as the wildly successful musical *Oklahoma!*

▲ Two sculptures by Oklahoma artist Allan Houser refer to the state's Native American history. *Sacred Rain Arrow (left)* can be seen at the Gilcrease Museum in Tulsa, while *As Long as the Waters Flow (right)* stands in front of the state capitol in Oklahoma City.

Numbering among Oklahoma's many famous writers are Tony Hillerman (author of *Sacred Clowns* and many other books); Pulitzer-winning Native-American writer N. Scott Momaday (author of *House Made of Dawn*); historian Daniel Boorstin (author of *The Creators*, *The Discoverers*, and other books); novelist Ralph Ellison (author of *Invisible Man*); and historian John Hope Franklin (author of *From Slavery to Freedom: A History of Negro Americans,* among other important works). Numerous prominent Oklahomans have written autobiographies about their early years in the Sooner State, including noted journalist Marquis James, cowboy humorist Will Rogers, and folk troubadour Woody Guthrie.

▲ The Rodgers and Hammerstein musical *Oklahoma!* in a 1979 Broadway revival. The musical includes such well-known songs as "Oh, What a Beautiful Mornin'," "Surrey With the Fringe on Top," and "The Farmer and the Cowman."

## Sports

Despite the absence of professional sports teams in Oklahoma, Sooners are still very sports-minded, focusing their competitive ardor on college teams such as the University of Oklahoma Sooners. Legendary collegiate football coach Bud Wilkinson led the Sooners to Big Eight Conference championships twelve consecutive times, beginning in 1947, winning three national titles.

Oklahoma has produced more than its share of professional sports athletes, including baseball greats Johnny Bench, Mickey Mantle, and Pepper Martin. Football star and

Olympian Jim Thorpe, regarded by some as history's greatest athlete, was from Oklahoma. Among the other pro football heroes who hail from the state are Troy Aikman and Brian Bosworth. Gymnast Shannon Miller, wrestler John W. Smith, and boxer Tommy Morrison number among Oklahoma's other sports champions.

## Ride 'em

Oklahomans are great rodeo fans. More than one hundred such events are held throughout the state annually, from high school competitions to those on the professional level. Oklahoma City's annual International Finals Rodeo is one of the sport's premier events. Rodeo star Jim Shoulders entered his first rodeo at the age of fourteen in his native Oklahoma. He was inducted into the National Cowboy Hall of Fame in 1956.

## Outdoor Oklahoma

Oklahoma has fifty state parks and a number of national wildlife refuges. The Salt Plains National Wildlife Refuge in north-central Oklahoma is a popular spot for birders. Bald eagles, pelicans, and sandhill cranes are among the hundreds of breeds of birds that visit the 32,000-acre (12,950-ha) site throughout the year. The Washita

### Sooners Let Their Babies Grow Up To Be Cowboys

Established in 1965, the National Cowboy and Western Heritage Museum in Oklahoma City was the brainchild of Kansas City businessman Chester A. Reynolds. Reynolds conceived the museum as a way to pay tribute to the brave pioneers who settled the West.

▼ The International Youth Rodeo in Shawnee showcases young talent and traditional skills.

Battlefield National Historic Site in western Oklahoma was the site of a violent clash between troops of the U.S. government, led by General George Custer, and a group of Southern Cheyenne in 1868. Located on the eastern border with Arkansas, the Fort Smith National Historic Site commemorates the period when Oklahoma was Indian Territory. It is also the site where the infamous "hanging judge," Isaac Parker, presided over local cases for twenty-one years.

Osage Hills State Park in the northeast was once an Osage settlement and is now a wooded park with a lake and campsites. Beavers Bend State Park in the southeast is on Broken Bow Lake in the Ouachita Mountains. Visitors can enjoy fishing, watching for eagles, and camping and hiking in the mountain wilderness. In the northwest, Alabaster Caverns State Park gives visitors a chance to explore underground Oklahoma in one of the largest known caverns made of alabaster. Five different species of bats make their home in the cave, and multicolored rock formations called selenites decorate the walls.

## Museums

The history of the Sooner State is preserved and displayed in dozens of public and private museums. The state-sponsored Oklahoma Historical Society directs the exhibits and activities of many regional museums. Anadarko is home to the Southern Plains Indian Museum and Crafts Center and Indian City U.S.A., where the dwellings of numerous Plains Indians groups can be viewed. One of the world's most extensive collections of Native American blankets is displayed at the Woolaroc Museum near Bartlesville.

The Will Rogers Memorial Museum is located in Claremore, where the famous cowboy philosopher and humorist grew up. In Lawton, the Museum of the Great Plains maintains informative exhibits on Native American history and culture. Oklahoma City is home to a wide variety of museums, including the Kirkpatrick Science and Air Space Museum. The educational exhibits here are designed for hands-on enjoyment. Oklahoma City also hosts the

▼ This tepee display at the Southern Plains Indian Museum and Crafts Center in Anadarko took place during an American Indian Exposition that celebrated the modern practice of traditional arts and crafts.

Oklahoma State Museum of History and the National Cowboy and Western Heritage Museum, which showcases the art and artists of the American West — and is also home to the Hall of Great Western Performers, the Hall of Great Westerners, and the Rodeo Hall of Fame. Tulsa boasts the Gilcrease Museum, which has an impressive collection of material relating to Native American history and art, and the Philbrook Museum of Art, where the collection includes Asian artwork and paintings by Italian Renaissance masters.

## Native Oklahoma

The Native American communities of Oklahoma host a number of events each year that celebrate tribal identity and traditional arts. The Cherokee National Holiday festival takes place in Tahlequah each year at the end of August. The festival celebrates the 1839 adoption of the Cherokee constitution and draws more than eighty thousand attendees. It also provides an occasion for people to meet up with old friends and enjoy performances of traditional dances as well as events such as a fishing derby, a golf tournament, and a dramatic interpretation of the Trail of Tears. The State of the Nation address is delivered each year at the National Holiday by the Cherokee Nation's principal chief.

The Choctaw, Sauk and Fox, and Pawnee Nations all hold annual powwows in the state, featuring traditional dance contests. For more than seventy years, the American Indian Exposition in Anadarko has been showcasing traditional and modern arts and crafts of Native Americans. Museums that celebrate tribal culture include the Cherokee Heritage Center in Tahlequah and the Five Civilized Tribes Museum in Muskogee.

▶ *Canyon Princess*, a sculpture by Gerald Balciar, is on display at the National Cowboy and Western Heritage Museum in Oklahoma City. This sculpture of a female cougar is twice life-size and celebrates western wildlife.

# People of Plain Distinction

> Up ahead they's a thousan' lives we might live,
> but when it comes, it'll on'y be one.
> — *Ma Joad, in* The Grapes of Wrath, *by John Steinbeck, 1939*

**Following are only a few of the thousands of people who were born, died, or spent much of their lives in Oklahoma and made extraordinary contributions to the state and the nation.**

## WILL ROGERS

### HUMORIST AND ACTOR

**BORN:** *November 4, 1879, near Oologah*
**DIED:** *August 15, 1935, near Point Barrow, AK*

**W**illiam Penn Adair Rogers is best remembered for his gentle humor and his witty, folksy commentaries on current events. Part Cherokee, Rogers grew up on a ranch, attended military school, then transported pack animals from Buenos Aires, Argentina, to South Africa for use in the Boer War (1899–1902). In South Africa, he performed rope tricks at Wild West shows and then began a New York City vaudeville career in 1905. Within about ten years, his stage persona of a plainspoken cowboy who skewered the fashionable attitudes of the day had made him a Ziegfeld Follies star. His popular daily syndicated newspaper column debuted in 1922, and he starred in such films as *They Had to See Paris* (1929) and *A Connecticut Yankee* (1931). Rogers became so popular that he was once nominated for governor of Oklahoma, although he declined to run. Among Rogers's books are *Rogersisms: The Cowboy Philosopher on Prohibition* (1919) and *The Illiterate Digest* (1924). During the Depression, Rogers worked to raise money for drought and flood victims. A promoter of aviation, he died in a plane crash.

DEDICATION
*Will Rogers*
FIELD
OKLAHOMA CITY
JUNE 28, 1941

# JIM THORPE
## ATHLETE

**BORN:** *May 28, 1887, near Prague*
**DIED:** *March 28, 1953, Lomita, CA*

**J**ames Francis Thorpe is widely regarded as the greatest athlete of the first half of the twentieth century. Thorpe, who was of Native American, French, and Irish ancestry, played football at the Carlisle Indian School in Pennsylvania, becoming an All-American in 1911 and 1912. At Carlisle, Thorpe also participated in baseball, lacrosse, and track. Thorpe set records in the 1912 Olympic Games, winning both the decathlon and the pentathlon. A year later, his gold medals were taken from him when it became known that Thorpe had been paid to play semiprofessional baseball and was therefore not technically an amateur athlete. Thorpe began his professional football career in 1915 with the Canton, Ohio, Bulldogs. From 1913 until 1919, he also played major league baseball. Thorpe became a charter inductee of the Pro Football Hall of Fame in 1963. The International Olympic Committee posthumously restored his gold medals in 1982.

# CHESTER GOULD
## CARTOONIST

**BORN:** *November 20, 1900, Pawnee*
**DIED:** *May 11, 1985, Woodstock, IL*

**C**hester Gould was an American cartoonist whose best-known creation is the long-running adventure comic strip *Dick Tracy.* Gould originated the strip in 1931 for the *Chicago Tribune,* but it quickly became popular across the country, thanks to national syndication. By some accounts, Gould based the strip's square-jawed hero on J. Edgar Hoover, the longtime director of the Federal Bureau of Investigation (FBI). *Dick Tracy* was peopled with a recurring cast of oddball villains, such as Pruneface and Flattop. Its message that "Crime Does Not Pay" endeared it to a regular readership of millions during the gangster-plagued years of the 1930s.

# WOODY GUTHRIE
## FOLK MUSICIAN

**BORN:** *July 14, 1912, Okemah*
**DIED:** *October 3, 1967, Queens, NY*

**T**he composer of more than one thousand songs, Woodrow Wilson Guthrie is considered by many to be the finest folk poet and folk musician who ever lived. He left home as a teenager, and, in 1935, he joined the "Okies" who fled from the Dust Bowl to California, working along the way as a migrant laborer and wandering musician. During this period, he composed many of his most powerful songs about social injustice and the plight of America's working people, including the classic "So Long, It's Been Good to Know You." Many of Guthrie's compositions were written in support of such causes as labor unions, President Franklin Roosevelt's Depression-era New Deal programs, and the Allied effort to win World War II. His most famous song is the beloved "This Land Is Your Land." Guthrie's laid-back and ironic style strongly influenced the folk singers of the early 1960s, including Joan Baez, Bob Dylan, Phil Ochs, and Tom Paxton. His son Arlo and his daughter Nora keep the Guthrie family folk-music tradition alive today.

# RALPH ELLISON
## WRITER

BORN: *March 1, 1914, Oklahoma City*
DIED: *April 16, 1994, New York, NY*

**R**alph Waldo Ellison's first novel, *Invisible Man* (1952), thrust him into the international spotlight and won the 1953 National Book Award for fiction. The novel portrayed an African-American man's quest for identity in a world in which the roles played by African Americans were largely determined by whites. While attending the Tuskegee Institute in Alabama (1933–1936), Ellison studied music, but his exposure to modern literature there convinced him to pursue a writing career instead. He relocated to New York City in 1936, where he joined the Federal Writers' Project and published essays and short stories in *New Challenge, New Masses,* and other magazines. After publishing *Invisible Man*, Ellison lectured extensively on African-American culture at colleges and universities across the nation, and he published short stories and essays. At the time of his death, he was writing a second novel. Ellison's short-story collection *Flying Home: And Other Stories* was discovered after his death and was published in 1996.

# MARIA TALLCHIEF
## BALLERINA

BORN: *January 24, 1925, Fairfax*

**E**lizabeth Marie Tall Chief was born to an Osage father and Scots-Irish mother in rural Osage County. She began taking dance lessons when she was three years old. Tall Chief studied with the famous Russian choreographer Bronislava Nijinska and also at the School of American Ballet. She shortened her name to Maria Tallchief when she began performing professionally. In 1942, she joined the Ballet Russe de Monte Carlo, where she quickly became a soloist. From 1946 to 1952, Tallchief was married to George Balanchine, the famous ballet choreographer, who created many of his best-known roles for her. As a dancer, she had a tremendous range and was able to play a wide variety of roles. In 1953, U.S. president Dwight Eisenhower declared her "Woman of the Year." She was given the title Wa-Xthe-Thomba, or "Woman of Two Worlds," by the governor of Oklahoma in the same year. From 1947 to 1965, Tallchief danced with the New York City Ballet. She retired in 1965 and, in 1981, founded the Chicago City Ballet with her sister, Marjorie, who was also a ballet dancer.

# THOMAS STAFFORD
## ASTRONAUT

BORN: *September 17, 1930, Weatherford*

**T**homas Patten Stafford was the U.S. astronaut in command of *Apollo 10*, the final test mission before the first manned lunar landing. A 1952 graduate of the U.S. Naval Academy, Stafford transferred to the Air Force and in 1962 was picked for the astronaut corps. With astronaut Walter M. Schirra, he flew into orbit on December 15, 1965, aboard *Gemini 6*, which had a rendezvous in space with *Gemini 7*, the first such maneuver ever performed. Stafford returned to space on June 3, 1966, commanding *Gemini 9*, which performed rendezvous and docking maneuvers, preparatory to the Apollo lunar missions. Stafford then commanded *Apollo 10*, launched moonward on May 18, 1969. During this mission, Stafford flew the lunar module *Snoopy* within 50,000 feet (15,240 m) of the lunar surface. Stafford's final space mission was as commander of the U.S. portion of the Apollo-Soyuz Test Project, launched in July 1975. This first-ever international space mission brought U.S. and Soviet crews together in orbit.

## MICKEY MANTLE
### BASEBALL PLAYER

BORN: *October 20, 1931, Spavinaw*
DIED: *August 13, 1995, Dallas, TX*

Mickey Charles Mantle became center fielder for the New York Yankees in 1951, playing in that position and at first base through the 1968 season. Overcoming frequent injuries, Mantle led the American League several times in runs scored, walks, and home runs. He won baseball's Triple Crown in 1956, finishing the season with a .353 batting average, 52 homers, and 130 RBIs (runs batted in); and he was voted the American League's

Most Valuable Player. He also won the award in 1957 and 1962. Mantle's hitting and fielding helped the Yankees win twelve pennants and seven World Series, in which he netted a record 18 home runs, 42 runs, 40 RBIs, and 43 walks. Mantle finished his career with 536 home runs, 1,734 walks, 2,415 hits, 1,677 runs scored, 1,509 RBIs, and a .298 batting average. He was inducted into the Baseball Hall of Fame in 1974, the first year in which he was eligible.

## WILMA MANKILLER
### SOCIAL REFORMER

BORN: *November 18, 1945, Tahlequah*

Wilma Pearl Mankiller was the first female chief of the Cherokee Nation. She spent her early years on an Oklahoma farm with her parents and ten siblings, but after a severe drought threatened their livelihood, the Bureau of Indian Affairs relocated the family in 1957 to a low-income Native American housing project in San Francisco, California. Mankiller was drawn to the Native American rights movement in 1969 when Native Americans occupied San Francisco's Alcatraz Island. She returned to Oklahoma in the mid-1970s, where she became economic stimulus coordinator for the Cherokee Nation in 1977, focusing on improving the tribe's prospects for education, employment, health care, and housing. In 1983, she was elected the Cherokee Nation's first female deputy chief. When the principal chief, Ross Swimmer, left in 1985, Mankiller became the Cherokee Nation's chief. She was elected in her own right in 1987 and 1991.

# Oklahoma

## History At-A-Glance

**1541**
Francisco Vásquez de Coronado and Hernando de Soto, working separately, begin exploring present-day Oklahoma.

**1817**
U.S. troops establish Fort Smith in eastern Oklahoma.

**1834**
The U.S. Congress establishes Indian Territory in eastern Oklahoma.

**1872**
The Missouri-Kansas-Texas Railroad, the first to cross Oklahoma, opens.

**1889**
President Benjamin Harrison opens Indian land to settlers.

**1893**
Oklahoma's biggest land run occurs on September 16, when more than one hundred thousand settlers rush into the Cherokee Outlet.

**1812**
The U.S. Congress incorporates the lands west of the Mississippi River, including Oklahoma, into the Missouri Territory.

**1830–42**
The U.S. government relocates the Five Civilized Tribes to Oklahoma via the "Trail of Tears."

**1861**
About six thousand Oklahoma Native Americans side with the Confederacy during the Civil War.

**1879–1880s**
"Boomers" pressure the federal government to allow white settlement in Oklahoma's Indian lands.

**1890**
The U.S. Congress establishes the Oklahoma Territory.

**1897**
Oklahoma's first high-volume oil well is drilled.

---

**1600**          **1700**          **1800**

---

**1492**
Christopher Columbus comes to New World.

**1607**
Capt. John Smith and three ships land on Virginia coast and start first English settlement in New World — Jamestown.

**1754–63**
French and Indian War.

**1773**
Boston Tea Party.

**1776**
Declaration of Independence adopted July 4.

**1777**
Articles of Confederation adopted by Continental Congress.

**1787**
U.S. Constitution written.

**1812–14**
War of 1812.

# United States

## History At-A-Glance

MILLER BRO

**1907**
The Twin Territories enter the Union together as Oklahoma, the nation's forty-sixth state.

**1910**
Oklahoma City is made the state's permanent capital. African Americans are legally prohibited from voting in Oklahoma.

**1921**
African Americans hold an anti-lynching rally in Tulsa; a riot ensues, during which about three hundred African Americans die.

**1928**
The Oklahoma City oil field is discovered and opened for drilling.

**1948**
U.S. Supreme Court orders equal educational opportunities for all Oklahomans regardless of color.

**1953**
Construction is completed on the Turner Turnpike, which connects Oklahoma City and Tulsa.

**1964**
Oklahoma's segregation laws overturned after African American-led protests.

**1970**
The McClellan-Kerr Arkansas River Navigation System is completed, allowing access to the Gulf of Mexico.

**1988**
Remington Park horse-racing track opens in Oklahoma City. The state enacts sweeping educational reforms.

**1990**
Oklahoma becomes the first state to institute term limits on its lawmakers.

**1995**
A domestic terrorist's bomb destroys the Alfred P. Murrah Federal Building in Oklahoma City, killing 168.

**1999**
About forty tornadoes strike Oklahoma, causing massive destruction.

**1800**    **1900**    **2000**

**1848**
Gold discovered in California draws eighty thousand prospectors in the 1849 Gold Rush.

**1861–65**
Civil War.

**1869**
Transcontinental railroad completed.

**1917–18**
U.S. involvement in World War I.

**1929**
Stock market crash ushers in Great Depression.

**1941–45**
U.S. involvement in World War II.

**1950–53**
U.S. fights in the Korean War.

**1964–73**
U.S. involvement in Vietnam War.

**2000**
George W. Bush wins the closest presidential election in history.

**2001**
A terrorist attack in which four hijacked airliners crash into New York City's World Trade Center, the Pentagon, and farmland in western Pennsylvania leaves thousands dead or injured.

▼ The diverse cast of a Wild West show near Ponca City in 1927.

# Festivals and Fun for All

**Check web site for exact date and directions.**

fifty bull riders against the fiercest bucking bulls on the pro rodeo circuit. At stake is $100,000 in prize money. Bullnanza is televised on The National Network (TNN). www.lazye.com/arena

### Guthrie Jazz Banjo Festival, Guthrie

Late in May, banjo players assemble from all over the state, performing concerts on up to eight separate stages. Among the attractions are a concert featuring the World's Largest Banjo Band, composed of more than 150 banjo players, a musical parade, a Banjo Hall of Fame banquet and induction ceremony, and a Sunday church service offering banjo music. The event concludes with a patriotic salute to the Sooner State's veterans. www.banjofestival.com

### Oklahoma State Fair, Oklahoma City

Held in September, the State Fair is the largest annual event of its kind in the state, offering agricultural exhibits, concerts and other entertainment, food, motorsports, and rodeo events. www.oklafair.org

### OkMozart Festival, Bartlesville

Each June, the hills of northeastern Oklahoma resound for nine days with the strains of the music of Wolfgang Amadeus Mozart. For nearly two decades, this event has produced concerts by such world-class performers as Joshua Bell, Branford Marsalis, Garrick Ohlsson, the Borromeo String Quartet, and the Los Angeles Guitar Quartet. The festival includes both indoor and outdoor concert venues. www.okmozart.com/default.asp

### American Indian Exposition, Anadarko

So many Plains Indian populations have lived in Anadarko that it is known as the nation's Native American capital. The city is now home to seven tribes. Each August, the town hosts the weeklong American Indian Exposition (*above*), a celebration of Native American dance, music, and food. Also featured are an all-Native rodeo and a historical pageant. www.usaindianinfo.org/expo.htm

### Bullnanza, Guthrie

Each February, Bullnanza, a two-day bull-riding spectacular, comes to the old Sooner capital of Guthrie. Sanctioned by Professional Bull Riders, Inc., this prestigious event pits the association's top

### Pawnee Bill's Wild West Show, Pawnee

Beginning in June, Pawnee Bill's Wild West Show runs on weekends throughout the summer, providing an exciting and entertaining living history lesson that the entire family can enjoy. The show is named for its late founder, Gordon "Pawnee Bill" Lillie, who had a Wild West show at the start of the twentieth century.
www.cowtowncoliseum.com/pawnee.asp

### Pioneer Days, Guymon

During the first weekend in May, the city of Guymon honors its frontier heritage with a parade, dancing, an arts-and-crafts show, and a rodeo.
www.guymoncofc.com /default.html

### Red Earth Native American Cultural Festival, Oklahoma City

This authentic Native American powwow convenes each June and is open to the public. The festival boasts the nation's largest gathering of Native American dancers and visual artists, with representatives of some one hundred Native American tribes present.
www.redearth.org/RE.htm

### Robbers Cave Fall Festival, Wilburton

Held on the third Friday, Saturday, and Sunday in October since 1998, the annual Robbers Cave Fall Festival offers arts and crafts, entertainment, a quilt show, a carnival, food vendors, a car show, and more.
www.wilburton.ok.us/calendar.html

### Rodeo and Old Cowhand Reunion, Freedom

Held in mid-August, this rodeo event also includes a dance, a "chuck-wagon feed," an arts-and-crafts fair, and a live-action re-creation of the Wild West entitled "The Great Freedom Bank Robbery and Shootout."
www.shopoklahoma.com/fest3q02.htm

### Sauk and Fox Nation Powwow, Stroud

Held in mid-July, this annual outdoor festival welcomes visitors as well as members of the Sauk and Fox tribes. The spotlight is on traditional Native American crafts, food, and dance competitions during this multi-day event.
www.shopoklahoma.com/fest3q02.htm

### Will Rogers Days, Claremore and Oologah

Held in early November in and around Rogers's birthplace, this weekend event features a parade, an arts-and-crafts festival at the Claremore Expo Center, and other activities at the Will Rogers Memorial Museum in Claremore and at the Will Rogers Birthplace Ranch in Oologah.
www.americanprofile.com/issues/20011014/20011014cen_1410.asp

### Woody Guthrie Folk Music Festival, Okemah

Folk musicians from across the nation gather in Okemah's Pastures of Plenty during the middle of each July to celebrate the life and artistry of America's most influential folk singer and composer.
www.shopoklahoma.com/fest3q02.htm

▼ *Riding Into the Sunset*, a statue by Electra Waggoner, stands at the Will Rogers Memorial Museum in Claremore.

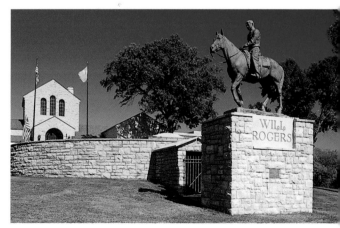

## Books

Antle, Nancy. *Beautiful Land: A Story of the Oklahoma Land Rush*. New York: Viking, 1994. A history of the Sooner State's tumultuous land-boom period.

Coombs, Karen Mueller. *Woody Guthrie: America's Folksinger*. Minneapolis, MN: Carolrhoda Books, 2002. The story of Woody Guthrie's life is both the story of an American genius and that of a whole generation of Oklahomans who struggled through the Dust Bowl days.

Hesse, Karen. *Out of the Dust*. New York: Scholastic, 1997. In this dramatic novel, 14-year-old narrator Billie Joe tells of her life in Oklahoma during the Dust Bowl years, bringing home the rugged realities of that difficult time.

Santella, Andrew. *The Cherokee*. New York: Children's Press, 2001. The Cherokee people have a long and fascinating history and unique way of life, described in this comprehensive and up-to-date book.

Updyke, Rosemary Kissinger. *Jim Thorpe, the Legend Remembered*. Gretna, LA: Pelican Publishing, 1997. The life story of the Oklahoma Native American, one of the most accomplished athletes who ever lived.

Wallis, Michael, with photographs by David Fitzgerald. *Oklahoma Crossroads*. Portland, OR: Graphic Arts Center Publishing Co., 1998. A picture-filled tour of the Sooner State.

## Web Sites

▶ Official state web site
www.state.ok.us

▶ Official web site of Oklahoma City, the state capital
www.okc-cityhall.org

▶ Oklahoma Historical Society web site
www.ok-history.mus.ok.us

▶ Official web site of Oklahoma's leading newspaper, the *Daily Oklahoman*, and an Oklahoma television station
www.newsok.com

Note: Page numbers in *italics* refer to maps, illustrations, or photographs.